ISBN: 978-1-909833-34-0
ISBN: 978-1-909833-30-2 (ePub)
ISBN: 978-1-909833-31-9 (MobiPocket)

www.themulberrycollection.co.uk

Dedication

This book is dedicated to

Ben, Matthew

Caspar, Sebastian

Thomas, Freddie

& Harry

'I flourish in light and in Shade'

The Author

Patricia (Aldridge) Irvine was born and brought up in a village at the heart of the Romney Marsh in Kent. A blissful childhood there helped to ensure that the Romney Marsh has always been an area of great inspiration in her two main passions of writing and photography.

In 2004 Patricia travelled to China to visit a relative of her late husband and whilst there she was approached to help record a book for the Sichuan University. At the end of the project, Patricia was invited to write and record a book of Children's verse, with the aim of helping Chinese children to learn English; and so "The Mulberry Collection - Book of Children's English Poetry and Chinese translations' was published in China in 2005.

For more information about Patricia and the inspiration behind her work, as well as her collection of poetry, children's fiction and photographic canvases, please visit www.themulberrycollection.co.uk.

The Illustrator

Kate Scurfield has drawn for corporate media clients for many years since a career move from chartered surveyor drew her into the cartoonists' world of publication. Readers of Horse & Hound and Polo Times amongst others have enjoyed the many detailed interpretations of their current affairs.

Kate was encouraged to draw from an early age using scrap paper her father, an engineer, brought home from work. His technical drawing skills, coupled with his enthusiasm, persuaded his daughter to follow her goal to become a popular and reliable contributor to major equestrian publications.

Numerous private clients have been immortalised in watercolour for special occasions. One of Kate's early assignments was illustrating a serial story for the publication Horse & Pony; now Kate returns to illustration providing images for a children's book of poems written by long-term friend and poet Patricia Irvine.

THE MULBERRY COLLECTION
(Words & Images)

FIRST BOOK
OF CHILDREN'S RHYMES

CONTENTS

www.themulberrycollection.co.uk

MY KITE!

My kite, is colourful and bright
I planned what I would do, one night
Next time we travel out of town
I'll find a piece of open ground
To fly my kite...

On the next bank holiday
I decided, I must find a way
And walked with friends and family
To open ground with nearby trees
To launch my kite...

The wind was strong and sure for me
Kite quickly soared above the trees
And in my mind I clearly saw
The many scenes...Kite's eyes, then saw
I **was** my kite!

I soared above those tallest trees
On the ground, people…small as bees
I danced in freedom with the clouds
Bursting with joy, I sang aloud
"I am my kite!"

We soared and dipped and floated there
"At One", with time and space and air
The colours clear as crystal jewels
Lakes and oceans…like tiny pools
"Fly high, my kite!"

Too soon, I heard within the crowd
My father's voice call out aloud
My freedom burst, feet on the ground
Once more, I was part of the crowd
"Pull in your kite!"

I wearily walked…back to home
Longing, for when I'd be alone…
In bed, I'd close my eyes and dream
Re-living every single scene

My Freedom – My Kite!

GOLDFISH IN A BOWL

I have a goldfish in a bowl
I could stare at him all day
I do believe he misses me
When I run out to play

I often find I talk to him
No words - just with my mind
I do believe he answers back!
With words gentle and kind

I lay out flat upon the floor
My head, on hands, is raised
I simply stare into his bowl
And he returns my gaze

I watch his gentle 'fishy' motion
And our souls are so entwined...
Silently, we exchange our stares
And there's a meeting of our
minds

To him, I tell my deepest secrets
And my hopes and dreams abound
I bare the very core of me
Yet, I never make a sound

I gaze in silent awe at him
As he circles round and round
I'm grateful for his silence
What loyalty I've found!

I can tell my fish just anything
Without ever knowing fear
My fish, I trust completely
This friendship's very dear

We often sit and gaze as one
Into each other's lives we peer
My goldfish...is my closest friend
And he remains my friend
All year!

GRANDMOTHER'S CATS

My Grandmother has seven cats
The first, is large and round and fat

The second cat, is small and thin
And when they race it always wins

The third cat's fur, is soft to touch
Although he doesn't like it much!

The fourth cat's eyes are really green
This cat will always steal the cream

The fifth cat, is my special cat
I play with him upon the mat

The sixth cat, is his young brother
And the seventh cat?

Their mother!

7

FIREWORKS

Fingers of colour...reach way up high
Forming magic spirals in the sky

Red and gold, silver and green
All of these so clearly seen

Their eerie screams make me jump with fright
As they shriek and soar throughout the night

With fingers stuffed in ears, I gaze
In breathless wonder through the haze

Cascades of purple, yellow and blue
Explosive bursts with a shimmering hue

My eyes drink in the amazing scene
The sky, a giant coloured screen

8

SHARING

We share the same sun, you and I
Me on the river
You in the desert
Beneath our umbrella of sky

We share the same moon, you and I
Me in the country
You in the city
Beneath our umbrella of sky

We share the same stars, you and I
I in the East
And you in the West
Still the same...umbrella of sky

We've so much to share, you and I...
We each have something to learn
And then something to teach
So, let's begin...
And give it a try!

10

FATHER'S CHICKENS

My father keeps some chickens
I have to feed them every day

I often am a little cross
When my friends run off to play!

It doesn't seem quite fair to me
That I work, whilst off they run

But I have to do it anyway
And cannot leave until it's done!

The chickens often try to peck
And they have such beady eyes...

The noise they make is very loud
(I think chickens - belong in pies!)

However...in the morning
My task I then complete

I love to collect the golden eggs
Which for breakfast - I can eat!

Chicken Pies

WATER

Splishing and splashing,
Then running cold and clear
The sound of water,
Is music to the ear

My mother's pots,
It makes bright and cool
And clothes it cleans,
For a day at school

With soap, it makes bubbles;
I must mind my eye!
If bubbles escape,
They float up to the sky

When the sky is angry
And thunder, loud
Fresh water falls,
Straight down from the cloud

Rivers happy and joyful,
Sparkle with light
Yet, lie quiet and dark,
Whilst I sleep at night

Fish will jump,
For the food that I hold
In summer, water,
Makes hot hands cold

The best water of all is, I think
Cold and delicious water to drink

SOIL

As a child, I would often play with soil
Carefully, for my clothes I dared not spoil!

Soft mud-clay pots I then would make
And place them in the sun to bake

With crumbling earth I'd fill the pots
Planting in each, small seeds like dots

From a watering can, each day I'd pour
Just the right amount; no less, no more

I watched keenly for the leaves to show
So anxious was I, to see them grow...

Then, day by day and hour by hour
I'd wait and watch to see them flower

On "Flowering Day" I felt such joy inside
I thought my heart would burst with pride

CANDLELIGHT

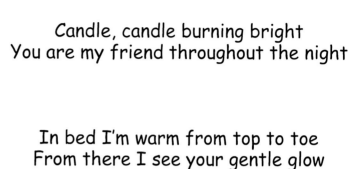

Candle, candle burning bright
You are my friend throughout the night

In bed I'm warm from top to toe
From there I see your gentle glow

I know that night, quite soon will end
Till then I'm safe with you my friend

17

When, at night, strange sounds I hear
I look at you and feel no fear

Candle, candle burning bright
You are my friend...throughout the night

THE WILD WIND

The wild wind howls and shrieks, throughout the night

Safe in my bed, I pull the covers tight!

It knocks at the door and raps at window panes

I bury deep...in bedcovers again!

It screams through the house and under the door

I clutch hold of my covers, once more!

At last…when the wind is quiet and sane

With joy, I return to my dreams again

THE ROOSTER

The Rooster is a noisy chap!
Whilst snug in bed, flat on your back

His morning call he will begin
It really is a **frightful** din!

His friends nearby, echo replies
We're forced to open tired eyes

Their cries declare, dawn has begun
It's time to rise before the sun

Perched on high before the dawning
He knows he's master of the morning!

Puffing out his chest, "I'm proud" he'll cry
As the morning chorus fills the sky

His feathers shine with colours bright
As he declares the end of night

He struts about upon stiff legs
Whilst calmly, *Hen*, lays golden eggs!

SIGNPOSTS IN THE SKY

Moon and stars are shining bright
Guiding us throughout the night

They are like signposts in the sky
When in our dreams we learn to fly

And higher than a giant kite
We travel fast throughout the night

And as we journey through our dreams
We're shown the most amazing scenes

Friends we meet - there are no foes!
All the while...our knowledge grows

When we reach the place, where dreams give birth
Then we're gently guided back to Earth

CHILDHOOD DREAMS

In the middle of a field I stand
Both feet firmly planted on the land

I look up, a great silver bird I see
Shining in the sky, flying over me

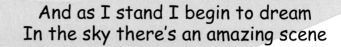

And as I stand I begin to dream
In the sky there's an amazing scene

A silver arc against deep blue skies
The sunlight's strong, so I shield my eyes

I dream of flying in this great bird
To far-off places, whose names I've heard

In schoolroom classes, with maps and plans
Of foreign people in distant lands

And as I stand there silently
I make a promise, just to ME!

At my lessons, I shall **really try**
So one day, I too, can learn to fly!

THE ANCHORAGE

I'd love to laze upon a yacht
With a gentle breeze
And the sun...hot

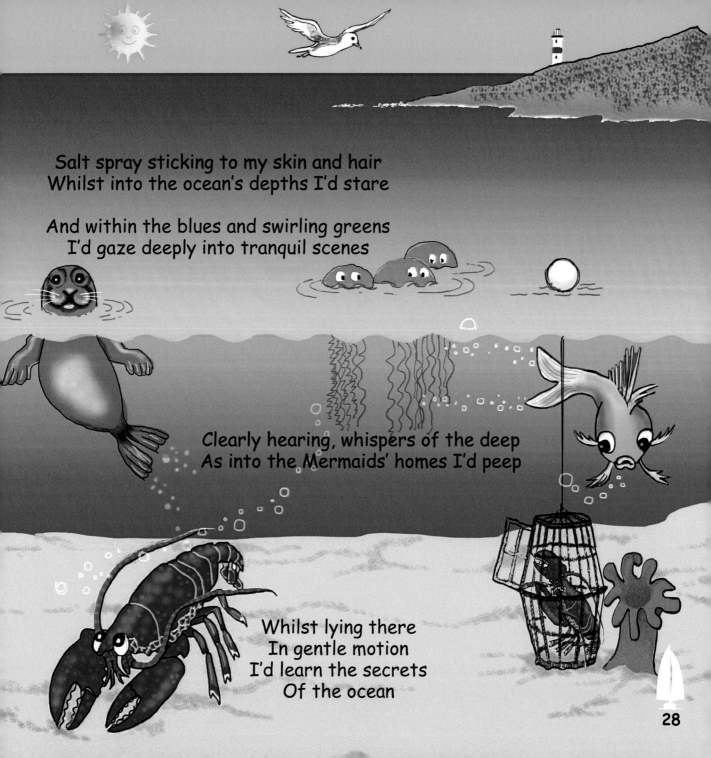

Salt spray sticking to my skin and hair
Whilst into the ocean's depths I'd stare

And within the blues and swirling greens
I'd gaze deeply into tranquil scenes

Clearly hearing, whispers of the deep
As into the Mermaids' homes I'd peep

Whilst lying there
In gentle motion
I'd learn the secrets
Of the ocean

FIRELIGHT DANCING

A winter night, in fireside seat

Beside the hearth, I toast my feet

I'm safe indoors, past setting sun

The 'firelight dancing' has begun

Peering into the flames I see

Tiny people, smiling back at me

Colours flicker before my eyes

Mystic folk...fly in changing skies

Orange, yellow, purple and blue

Fairies and elves, await their cue

There...dancing in the fire I see

Those magic scenes which are just for me!

WOODLAND FAIRIES

I ventured deep into the woods today
Tiny woodland fairies came out to play

They would flit from tree to tree
Playing 'Hide and Seek' with me

I decided to sit down on the ground
And not a movement made...nor any sound

Satisfied that the coast was clear
Those tiny folk, then reappeared

When happy and sure, they were safe once more
They danced together on the woodland floor

Swapping healing potions and magic spells
Gossiping and laughing like tinkling bells

HEALING POTIONS

STORY TIME

At story time,
They listened carefully
So enchanted were they,
No one noticed me!

SANDCASTLES

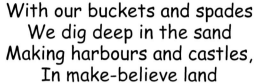

With our buckets and spades
We dig deep in the sand
Making harbours and castles,
In make-believe land

I am queen of the castle;
You're the captain at sea
When I find I'm in danger,
You'll rescue me!

Seashells we collect
Along the shore
We are 'sea-shell-rich';
We will **never** be poor!

Holes are dug deeper,
Turrets built high
My castle's tower
Will reach to the sky!

For hours and hours
On the beach we play
Making the most
Of a warm, sunny day

Tired and hungry,
Our energy spent
We wonder where
All the daytime went...

The tide has now turned
And will wash dreams away
But a blank canvas we'll have,
To begin the **next** day!

BALLOON'S PLAYTIME

I had a bright, new red balloon
Tied by ribbon to my wrist

It floated high up in the sky
I'm sure, the sun it kissed!

It danced and pranced
Among the clouds
And bounced
Both here and there

As it flounced
And pounced around
All I could do...was stare

When the wind joined in the game
I had to hold on really tight!

For as my balloon's excitement grew
It pulled with all its might

Soon...the wind grew tired
Its wild energy, was spent

But my balloon was joyful,
Happy and content

Softly, the daylight dimmed
The moon and stars came out to play

Wandering home, we saved some fun
To enjoy another day!

36

GRANDFATHER'S UMBRELLA

Grandfather gave me his bright umbrella
This soon became my friend
There must be a special reason
If my umbrella - I'm to lend!

It shields me from the storms
And the icy winter rain
In the heat of summer sun
It helps me once again

If I am in trouble
And friends, not on my side
By opening my umbrella
From them all...I'll hide!

If my ball lands in a tree
And I cannot reach it with a stick
I'll summon my umbrella
To perform his magic trick!

For...when I press a button
He will **double** in his size
Oh yes! My friend Umbrella
Is indeed a treasured prize!

When sometimes I am angry
Lose my temper and begin to shout
Umbrella shows me his displeasure
By turning inside out!

A TREASURE BOX

Today, I found a bright new acorn
And recently, a feather
I've decided I shall keep a box
Of things I want to treasure

I've added to my collection
A 'lucky' crystal stone
Lately, too, I came across
A fragrant, old pine cone

One day I found a rusty coin
Yes, I know it wasn't mine!
But Mother told me I could keep it
And I've really made it shine!

From the seashore...a lobster claw
And then, some brightly coloured shells
I'm sure that mermaids use them
When they chime their wedding bells.

I found a poppy head with seeds
And a length of golden string
My treasure box is overflowing...
And I'm as rich as any king!

MY STEAM ENGINE

When I grow up, I've decided, an engine driver I shall be
Yes, I think that fits the bill, I'm sure it's just the job for me!
I shall wear a large black hat with a long and pointed peak
You know, the one that looks just like a giant seagull's beak!

I shall wear dark overalls that are all covered in soot
With big, black shiny boots that will adorn each foot
Around my neck, I shall wear a bright yellow scarf
On this, I'll wipe my sooty face and that will make you laugh!

A red duster in my pocket will help to keep my engine clean
And as you see us coming closer, his paintwork will simply gleam!
I shall paint him bright blue; "Hurricane" will be his name
Nowhere, in the whole wide world, will an engine look the same!

The whistle will be noisy, to warn oncoming cars
It will be so very, very loud; they'll hear it, up on Mars!
My passengers will all be children, a trip with us they'll prize
Because this very special train, will be one-third the adult size!

All day I will keep busy, for I am so very keen
Together, with my engine's help, we'll work up a head of steam...
And as we puff along the track, flying faster than any bird
People, will gasp, and point, and say,
"That whistle's the best we've heard!"

At the end of each long day,
When it's time to go to bed
First, I'll make quite certain...
**My engine's tucked,
Safely, in his shed!**

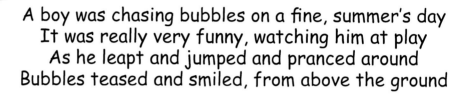

BUBBLES OF HOPE

A boy was chasing bubbles on a fine, summer's day
It was really very funny, watching him at play
As he leapt and jumped and pranced around
Bubbles teased and smiled, from above the ground

He whirled and spun, stretching with all his might
But he could not catch them in their dainty flight...
Those bubbles dazzled in the smiling sun
Translucent beauty, shone from every one

The boy laughed as he tried with shining eyes
To secure a glorious 'bubble' prize!
He chased those bubbles so blindly that
He fell, tripping over the neighbour's cat!

AND THEN HE STOPPED!

He spied from the corner of his eye
One bubble had settled ~ way up high
He scratched his head in disbelief
This bubble had settled on a leaf

His prize in sight, he reached gently out
And was ready to voice a triumphant shout
So he touched his prize ~ a glorious first!
But to his horror, it simply burst!

PROVING

Journeys are often far more fun
Than the moment we arrive
So, remember
Keep the hope in **your** heart

Fully alive!